MILLION DOLLAR PROFESSIONALISM FOR THE WRITER

To John—
Be a pro!

MILLION DOLLAR PROFESSIONALISM
FOR THE WRITER

Kevin J. Anderson
& Rebecca Moesta

WordFire Press
Colorado Springs, Colorado

MILLION DOLLAR PROFESSIONALISM FOR THE WRITER

The authors and publisher have strived to be as accurate and complete as possible in creating the Million Dollar Writing series. We don't believe in magical outcomes from our advice. We do believe in hard work and helping others. The advice in our Million Dollar Writing series is intended to offer new tools and approaches to writing. We make no guarantees about any individual's ability to get results or earn money with our ideas, information, tools or strategies. We do want to help by giving great content, direction and strategies to move writers forward faster. Nothing in this book is a promise or guarantee of future book sales or earnings. Any numbers referenced in this series are estimates or projections, and should not be considered exact, actual or as a promise of potential earnings. All numbers are for the purpose of illustration. The sole purpose of these materials is to educate and entertain. Any perceived slights to specific organizations or individuals are unintentional. The publisher and authors are not engaged in rendering legal, accounting, financial, or other professional services. If legal or expert assistance is required, the services of a competent professional should be sought.

ISBN: 978-1-61475-243-1

Cover design by Janet McDonald

Art Director Kevin J. Anderson

Cover artwork images by Dollar Photo Club

Book Design by RuneWright, LLC
www.RuneWright.com

Published by
WordFire Press, an imprint of
WordFire, Inc.
PO Box 1840
Monument CO 80132

Kevin J. Anderson & Rebecca Moesta, Publishers

WordFire Press Trade Paperback Edition October, 2014
Printed in the USA
wordfirepress.com

The Million Dollar Writing Series

When seeking advice, always consider the source. Many self-appointed "experts" write how-to books without themselves ever accomplishing the thing they are trying to teach you how to do.

In the Million Dollar Writing Series, each of our authors has sold a minimum of one million dollars of commercial product in their field. They have proved themselves, and here they share their wisdom, advice, and experience with you.

There are many factors in becoming a successful writer, and we cannot guarantee that you'll break into the top levels, but we hope you find the advice to be useful and enlightening.

CONTENTS

Introduction

If you want to be *treated as* a professional writer, you need to *act like* a professional. Take yourself and your career seriously. Behave in a way that you would expect a professional to behave.

When you see a doctor, lawyer, banker, or business executive, you expect certain standards—that they are mature, reliable people you'd want to do business with.

You've probably seen writers portrayed on TV or film as eccentric, ditzy, pompous, or curmudgeonly, as if that's the norm for a writer. They shrug. "Eh, *creative* people. What can you do?"

You can be professional.

When Kevin sold his first novel in 1987, he received an author questionnaire from the publisher's publicity department, asking about his interests, his areas of expertise, and his background in doing interviews and public appearances. Before the publisher turned him loose on book signings or set up media interviews, Kevin naïvely assumed that someone would *train* him. Since the publisher had a vested interest in their author making a good public impression, shouldn't they go over a list of guidelines or standards of behavior to make sure he was ready for prime time? After all, as an author representing their publishing company, he had their reputation as well as his own on the line. Surely they gave their authors some kind of code of conduct to keep them from shooting themselves in the foot, putting their foot in their mouths, or any other foot metaphor you prefer. When he asked about it, they told Kevin, "You should just know what to do."

Unfortunately, many authors have no idea what to do.

After a successful career spanning more than a quarter of a century, with over 125 books published and 50+ national or international bestsellers, Kevin has spent a lot of time learning how to be professsional.

He and his wife Rebecca—also an award-winning and *New York Times* bestselling author of dozens of books—have given lectures and workshops for thousands and thousands of writers.

They have presented their seminar "Things I Wish Some Pro Had Told Me When I Was Starting Out" for two decades, often to standing-room-only crowds.

Finally, they decided it was time to put that information in writing. The need for business knowledge and professional behavior is greater than ever. With more authors choosing the indie publishing route, they are forced to be front and center—producing and promoting their books, meeting fans, talking to bookstores. No longer can socially inept authors safely tuck themselves away in a cabin so they can write, while someone else does all the legwork.

With the explosion of social media, blogs, and discussion boards, where writers have direct interact-tions with readers—not to mention the potential for unfortunate flame-wars—it is imperative that writers learn to be professional, to stand out above the crowd of amateurs and be taken seriously.

The authors hope this book helps. They'll be watching.

PART I

THE PROFESSIONAL MINDSET

Speak, Dress, and Act Professionally

Writers aren't always dazzling socialites or the life of the party. In fact, writers tend to be more reclusive than average, maybe even a bit eccentric. They commute to fictional worlds for their daily work, and hang out with imaginary friends.

In the real world, though, a professional writer needs to adhere to certain basic social standards—such as grooming and hygiene. Don't laugh: we wouldn't be saying this if we hadn't met so many counter-examples.

If you're going to be in public, meeting editors, authors, and readers, follow these rules:

- Bathe
- Brush your teeth
- Wear clean clothes
- Look like someone an editor would want to do business with

Each time you talk to an editor or a publisher, whether it's at a cocktail party, on a panel, at lunch, or just chatting in the hall, think of it as a job interview. Yes, the vintage *Star Wars* t-shirt that you bought at the original showing of the film back in 1977 might be your favorite shirt, but—be honest with yourself—it's been laundered too many times and doesn't really fit all that well anymore. No, you don't have to wear a business suit (most authors don't), but at least look professional.

When an editor talks to you, she will form an immediate assessment from your first impression. *Is this a person I can rely on? Will this author deliver a book on time, as contracted, handle herself well in interviews, and appear at bookstore after bookstore without annoying the managers or customers? Is this somebody I want to work with?*

In public, Kevin generally wears a nice sport jacket, dress shirt, slacks, no tie (it's a challenge for him even to remember how to tie a necktie). It's a look that Rebecca has developed and cultivated for him, and it works.

O O O

Kevin

When I attended my very first swanky Nebula Awards ceremony in Oakland, California, I was seated at a table with a dashingly dressed Robert Silverberg and a similarly tuxedoed Dan Simmons. Much to my embarrassment, I actually did wear that old and faded Star Wars t-shirt mentioned above—and stuck out like a sore thumb. I looked like an amateur.

That was not the impression I wanted to make when sitting next to the titans of science fiction and fantasy.

Consider and create a specific look for yourself. Mega-bestseller Neil Gaiman never appears without his black leather jacket, black t-shirt, and aviator shades. Award-winning author Jay Lake and bestseller Aaron Allston were both well known for wearing bright Hawaiian shirts at every public appearance. Bestselling young adult author James A. Owen always wears a smart white shirt and black pants with a Victorian-looking vest, complete with pocket watch.

You might want to think through your branded look, though, before you choose something particularly elaborate. Bestselling dark fantasy author Sherrilyn Kenyon showed up at a large convention in a lovely crushed-velvet dress, corset, top hat, and gloves which gave her a beautiful steampunk appearance … in supremely humid and hot Atlanta in August; she told us she never wanted to do that again.

Speak Professionally

When you speak on stage or in public, even in hallway conversations, people will expect that a writer has a certain command of the language. Be articulate.

Use complete sentences. When people hear you talk, they should want to read your books.

You don't have to be prissy and erudite Professor Higgins from *My Fair Lady*, but you probably don't want to curse like a drunken sailor either—unless that's the brash, edgy image you're trying to project. (Even so, the longevity of brash, rude, in-your-face authors doesn't tend to be great.)

The same goes for online interactions. When people read a posting you made, they should not roll their eyes at poor grammar, sloppy spelling, or frequent typos. Instead, they should be impressed with how interesting you are, so they will want to seek out your blogs, articles, stories, or books.

Be Reliable

If you accept a writing assignment, do what you agreed to do, because someone is relying on you.

The publication process of a book or magazine or website involves a lot of moving pieces; don't be the sand that clogs up the gears.

Turn in your stories, columns, novels, scripts

- On time
- On topic
- At the correct length.

If you're the sort of writer who cannot operate that way—if you can't plan ahead, be bound by contracts, and deadlines, or subject or length constraints—then don't take the assignment in the first place. You'll just cause headaches for yourself and for everybody who is counting on you.

That's not to denigrate your skill as a writer, but to show courtesy to all the other people involved in the production process who need to get a job done. You'll be better off writing your works on spec, at your own pace; once the manuscript is finished to your satisfaction, then try to find a market for it.

If you agree to do a particular story for a particular anthology, then you have made a commitment to the editor. It's your obligation to do your part. Editors have deadlines too. They are expected to deliver the manuscript that the publisher contracted for. That editor is counting on you.

O O O

Kevin

I signed a contract with a major publisher to deliver a 100,000-word anthology based on a popular media property with stories about a specified list of characters.

Because these were all stories set in a well-defined, pre-established universe, I chose a group of fellow authors who were familiar with the series and the characters. They were also writers I thought I could work with. As colleagues, they had made a good impression on me when I got to know them. The publisher gave me a hard deadline when I had to turn in the completed manuscript with all the stories ready to go.

This was going to be a major title for the publisher, the lead release for that month. Advertising geared up in advance. Sales representatives solicited orders from bookstores across the country. The cover art was commissioned.

Each writer promised to deliver a 5,000 word story about their character. (Note: in fiction, a request for 5,000 words is usually an estimate, and a range of 4,000–6,000 words is acceptable). The authors signed contracts to deliver by a date that gave me enough time to read all the submissions, request rewrites if necessary, and then deliver the nice, neat package to the publisher. That way, everyone could plan for the book.

Because I had invited real professionals, the authors delivered their stories just as I requested. Exactly on time. All at the right length.

Except one.

As my deadline with the publisher approached, I began to sweat, still waiting for the last story. I nudged the author, who promised me that the story was coming. Two weeks later, still no manuscript, and everything else was done. The publisher was waiting. So I prodded the author again, this time with more enthusiasm. Yes, I was promised, it was almost done. The story was coming.

Now the publisher was starting to sweat. The anxious editor wanted to know where the anthology was; everyone was ready to go into production. The release date was coming up.

So, I begged and cajoled the delinquent author, even used a threatening tone. Now, this was not a story I could just leave out of the book; it was about an absolutely vital character. And by now it was much too late for me to find a replacement writer.

Finally, weeks after the publisher had expected the complete production manuscript, I received the story. And, no, it was not the agreed-upon 5,000 words, not even within the margin of error … but three times that length. 15,000 words!

"The story got out of hand," the writer told me. "But it's really good. You'll love it."

So, not only was the story delivered more than a month late, it was vastly longer than I had been expecting.

This caused more than one problem in the line of publication dominoes. When commissioning these stories from my fellow professional authors, I had offered them a pay rate of 5¢/word. Here's how it works: when a publisher contracts me to edit an anthology, they give me a certain amount of money to work with. The editor generally keeps half of the advance for her share and the remaining half is divided up among the authors. The editor budgets accordingly.

Expecting 5,000 word stories—which is what the authors had promised to deliver—I had divided up the advance money so I could pay for them all. But now, at the very end of the whole process, with everything else delivered and all the money paid out except for what I had budgeted for the maddeningly late author, I suddenly had to pay for three times as many words as I had anticipated!

Guess where that money comes from. The editor's share.

I was not happy with this.

But wait—there's more. The publisher had already been soliciting and advertising this title. They already had covers printed. Expecting a 100,000 word book, as had been contracted, they had the spine width set and an approximate number of pages. Therefore, they had established the book's cover price—at least until I dumped an extra 10,000 words on them. That dramatically changed the page count in the printed book—by 10%—and either forced them to raise the price of the book or reset the entire volume with smaller type so that it could fit in the same number of pages.

They were not happy with this, either.

I have edited many subsequent anthologies. That particular author did not ever receive a second invitation.

We have gotten much of our continued work in the publishing industry by proving that we are reliable and professional. Together, we wrote fourteen *Young Jedi Knights* books for Lucasfilm, which were released every three months, forty-two months in a row. Initially, they commissioned us for three books, then six, then eleven, then fourteen. If an editor knows he can count on you, that's one less thing for him to worry about.

When you prove that you are a reliable writer, you become a writer that the editor will work with again. And again.

Always Do Your Best Work

Everything you write and send out into the world via book, magazine, game, blog, newsletter, or other medium will be *some reader's* first encounter with your work. Every piece of work you publish is an audition for future readers. There is no such thing as an insignificant story.

Yes, sometimes deadlines are tight, and you won't have as much time to polish as you'd like, but still give your best effort in a given timeframe. Pour your focused energy into it. Don't ever "phone it in" and let yourself create less than your best.

O O O

Kevin

I was in Los Angeles teaching a writer's workshop and also frantically working on the last line edits to a novel manuscript that was just about to go into production. I absolutely had to FedEx the manuscript to the publisher no later than Saturday. I worked and reworked certain scenes, polishing up the descriptions to make them as good as possible.

Expecting to finish the book ahead of deadline, I made plans to spend that Saturday with a friend. We intended to go to Universal Studios, have lunch, enjoy the day. But by Friday night, I still wasn't satisfied with all the revisions I wanted to make on the novel.

I called my friend and postponed getting together with him until Saturday afternoon, because I needed several more hours to work on the manuscript. He was disappointed. "Come on, we'll have fun!" Even though I insisted that my editing took priority, he kept turning the thumbscrews. "Oh, you don't need to work so hard—and why does it matter? That's just a Star Wars novel! Who's going to know the difference?"

Just a Star Wars novel?

"This Star Wars novel is going to be read by hundreds of thousands of people," I said. "If I don't do my absolute best job, how can I expect those readers to try any of my other books?"

So, I spent Saturday morning polishing until I was satisfied, then shipped the manuscript off just before the FedEx pickup deadline. And in the afternoon I had fun with my friend.

That novel was Darksaber, *which became a big bestseller and is still voted by the fans as one of the best Star Wars novels ever written. I'm glad I spent the extra time and effort.*

No writing assignment is too trivial to deserve your best efforts. Once you commit to contribute, don't change your mind and decide the work is beneath you. If you accept an invitation to write a story for the Purple Unicorn Stories anthology, for instance, don't whine to your friends or fellow writers, "Oh, brother, I can't believe I have to do a lame story for a ridiculous Purple Unicorn Stories anthology. I mean, who *cares* about purple unicorns, anyway?"

By taking on the challenge, you have agreed to do the job and are *obligated to deliver your best work*. Regardless of what you think about the literary merits of purple unicorns, never forget that the people who buy a book of purple unicorn stories genuinely want to read and enjoy them. They are *paying* for that book. You owe them the best purple unicorn experience you can produce in the given timeframe. If you have a low opinion of your readers, they will sense your attitude. Conversely, if you do your best to deliver the best darn purple unicorn story possible, you will probably earn faithful readers for your other work.

Complaining about a job that you accepted is a demonstration of bad manners. When people (especially editors) hear you disparage a project, you come across as difficult or unpleasant to work with.

On the other hand, if you accept an assignment, do a good job, and act like a professional, it's likely that more work will come your way.

O O O

We have been giving workshops on professionalism for two decades, often using the purple unicorn example. In 2014, at the Superstars Writing Seminar in Colorado Springs, one of our other guest speakers was Lisa Mangum, the editor at a major publishing house. When she heard our lecture, she was so intrigued by the concept that she offered to edit the purple unicorn anthology, if we chose to do it.

Six months later, WordFire Press released *One Horn to Rule Them All: A Purple Unicorn Anthology*, with stories by Jody Lynn Nye, Todd McCaffrey, and Peter S. Beagle, as well as contributions from our writing graduates, with all profits going to a scholarship fund for the Superstars Writing Seminar.

And they are some truly exceptional purple unicorn stories!

Don't Be a Jerk

A professional writer acts professional.

If you want to be perceived as an author who deserves the respect of your peers, your editors and publishers, and your readers, then *be professional.* It's not just a façade you present when in public, it's a fundamental attitude that you carry with you wherever you go. It's the way you take on assignments, the way you treat other people in the workplace, and how you get your writing done.

Here's the first important lesson:

Never,

never, ever,

never, never, never, never, ever

be a jerk.

(There are alternate technical terms, many of them not fit for polite company.)

Never be a jerk. Not to anyone you interact with: assistants, editors, fans online, fans you meet face to face, fellow writers, reviewers, interviewers. In fact, while we're at it, never be a jerk to the cashier at the store either, or to the UPS driver, or to the appliance repair tech. Treating your fellow humans with respect is good for your karma, and it's just common decency.

But *other than decency*, why should a writer bother being nice to the gardener, or the gas station attendant?

Because everyone—*everyone*—is important. The possibilities are countless. The guy ahead of you in line at the post office might become a business associate. At a writer's conference, the person at the bar asking for more pretzels may be an editor, a publisher, a bookseller, or a fellow writer who could invite you into an anthology. The attorney you meet in a coffee shop might be willing to give you some pointers for a legal thriller you're writing. If nothing else, each person you meet is a potential reader or supporter of your work.

There's no drawback to being nice. That's what *professionals* do.

Throughout the year, we attend many science fiction conventions, pop-culture gatherings, and writer's conferences. We make every effort to be visible and personable. We go through the dealer's room, talk with the booksellers, offer to autograph any copies of our books they have for sale—even used books. A used book may be a reader's first introduction to your work, and if that reader enjoys the book, she might want to read (or buy) something else of ours. She may also recommend our books to her friends. We autograph any copy a fan brings, no matter how battered it might look.

What does it cost you? A few seconds of your time. But if you are rude, especially to a fan, then anecdotes about it will spread like wildfire across the internet. If you're a jerk, word gets around. The best way to avoid a bad reputation is to not be a jerk in the first place.

At a convention Kevin attended, a Big Name Author was standing outside the dealer's room when someone asked if he would go in and sign some of his books for the dealers. The author sniffed and said quite plainly, and within earshot of those book dealers, "Why should I bother? They're just tiny stores." As soon as he left, the dealers methodically removed his books from their shelves, stripped the paperbacks, and returned them for credit. If they carried his titles at all from that point forward, they certainly did it without enthusiasm.

The consequences of your actions can be unexpected. They might even remain invisible to you. In the case of this rude author, he may never have realized the damage he did to his reputation. But treating others well can also yield surprising reactions. Sometimes it may be years before you find out about your effect on others (if you find out at all). Here are a couple of examples.

We were attending the World Science Fiction Convention in Glasgow, Scotland, which was held at a large conference center some distance from the hotel. After checking into our hotel, we set off for the convention center to pick up our badges. When we hailed a cab in front of the hotel, another woman was standing there, also waiting. After long years of experience, we've learned how to spot science fiction fans, and this woman fit the bill. When a cab pulled up, Kevin asked her, "Are you going to Worldcon? Would you like to share a cab?" The woman was surprised and agreed. We rode together, talking all the way. This fan had never read any of our books, or even heard of us, but we had fun chatting on the way to the convention center. When we got there, we paid the tab for the taxi. The fan offered to split the fare, but we said no, since we had invited her to be our guest for the ride, and it hadn't cost any more to have her join us. She thanked us, and we went our separate ways.

About five years later, Kevin was doing a book signing at Powell's Books in Portland, Oregon. Among the people who showed up for the event was the woman from the taxi in Glasgow. She brought two large shopping bags filled with books. After introducing herself she said, "You were so nice to pick up that cab ride in Scotland that I looked up your books. I've bought every single title you ever published."

And she had. Kevin autographed them all.

In another case, we were doing an autographing at the Book Expo America in New York, a trade show that caters to booksellers. Kevin was a featured author, and as he was signing books, a couple came up to him in the line. "You probably don't remember us, but we own a very small book store in Sacramento, California. You signed your first novel, *Resurrection, Inc.*, for us when it first came out. Only five people showed up for the signing, and some authors would have been angry, but you took it in stride and were so pleasant that we remembered you. Since then, we've featured every one of your titles as they came out, and we give them prominent placement."

Everyone is important.

None of this could possibly have been planned. Being respectful of others is not part of some nefarious scheme to trick people into paying more attention to our books. It's the way professionals should treat anyone they meet.

Never, never, never be a jerk.

Don't Make Enemies or Start Feuds

As with Don't Be a Jerk, this is good advice for life in general.

In the tight-knit publishing world, everybody knows everyone. Don't criticize, embarrass, one-up, or denigrate *anyone*—either to their faces or behind their backs. Even if your agent's secretary didn't take a message properly. Even if you're upset about a person in your writing group who always tears down the stories you submit. Even if a critic totally misunderstood the plot of your novel and wrote a terrible review. Do not make enemies: it will come back to haunt you.

Even if a person really is as dimwitted as you think they are, it will not improve the world for you to point it out. Nobody will think better of you because of it.

And the very enemy you make by criticizing someone, might later end up being in a position to hurt your career. People pass the word. Writers, editors, and production staff move from one publisher to another.

Within a week they can change from having no power to having the power to buy or reject your work.

O O O

Rebecca

We attended a large writing conference at which Kevin was a guest speaker. At one of the main panels, he was on stage with seven other writers in a ballroom packed with about three hundred people in the audience. The moderator asked how writers should go about choosing their next project.

Kevin explained, "I have dozens of ideas for stories at any time, so I have plenty of options. When I decide my next project, I evaluate all those ideas and consider which one might appeal to the widest possible audience. Some ideas will fit only an obscure little niche, while others are crowd pleasers. For example, a story about an internally conflicted Bosnian bicycle repairman who is also a child abuser is not as likely to become a bestseller as, say, an amusement park with cloned dinosaurs."

The other panelists gave their own answers, and then one sneered down the table at Kevin. "I couldn't disagree more! He doesn't know what he's talking about." This author proceeded to verbally rip Kevin to shreds in a large room with hundreds of people watching. "A writer can only write what's in his or her heart, without considering popularity or marketability. You can't try to predict what people will or won't like. You have to wrench the words from your soul, and only that way can you be faithful to your art. The story must spring forth of its own volition, and only then will you write something that is worthy of being read. If you do that, readers will find you, no matter what the subject is."

And so on …

Then, after tearing Kevin several new orifices, the author turned to the next person, pointed toward Kevin, and whispered loudly enough for the front rows to hear, "Who is that guy, anyway?"

Not exactly professional behavior. At the time, the sneering author had no more than a few short stories published. Kevin had more than twenty novels in print with about seven million copies sold.

Fast forward several years. Kevin was editing an invitation-only anthology on a specific topic, and he had planned it out, wanting to fill very particular spots. Kevin had already invited professional, reliable authors for each story, though he often keeps one or two slots open for newer writers. One night, Kevin received a phone call from a stranger: "I heard about your anthology, and it sounds fascinating. I've got a great idea for a story! I've started researching it, and I think it would be a perfect fit for you. I'd really like to contribute."

You guessed it: This was the same author who had torn him to shreds in front of a large audience—a person who seemed to have no memory of the incident. But Kevin remembered it.

"I'm sorry," he said, "the anthology is full."

In fact, the anthology was full, but Kevin had made exceptions in the past—if he had good reason to do so. This author had given him no incentive to bend the rules. Why would he go out of his way to make room for a person who had demonstrated such unprofessional behavior in the past and would likely be difficult to work with?

Kevin isn't the type to hold a long-term grudge, but the other author had done nothing to earn his confidence or friendship.

Writers, especially newer writers, love to get involved in the politics of writers' organizations or online flame wars. That rarely has any benefit.

Sure, some authors have become successful by being provocative gadflies or standing on political soapboxes, offending half of their potential readership in order to rally the other half. Most of us can't afford to lose half of our readers, especially over political arguments that have nothing to do with our books. Don't give a reader any reason to steer clear of your work.

O O O

And don't correct critics. You won't impress anyone by trying to "call them out" in public. Maybe they did miss the point. Maybe they have an obvious ax to grind. Shrug it off.

Kevin's first *Star Wars* novel *Jedi Search* was savaged by an initial reviewer—who complained about every aspect of the book, before ending the review with, "But I never liked *Star Wars* anyway." So why would a person who didn't like *Star Wars* in the first place bother to review a *Star Wars* novel? Who knows? Since (by his own admission) he was not the target audience for *Jedi Search,* it felt unfair that he would judge the book. But Kevin had to shake it off. The review did not affect the sales. To date, *Jedi Search* has sold more than two million copies.

We've seen authors get into vigorous debates with critics. Unfortunately, even if the author is factually correct (e.g., the reviewer misunderstood key aspects of the book or got facts wrong) no one comes out of the conflict unscathed in the eyes of the observers. The defensive author may feel victorious, but in fact he just looks petty.

Rise above the fray.

Don't Begrudge Other Writers Their Success

Some authors are going to be more successful than you will ever be—probably a lot more successful. Deal with it. That doesn't diminish *your* accomplishments.

Don't begrudge others their successes. Complaining about some other writer's work is unprofessional. You look like a whiner. And a poor sport. It does *not* make you look like a better writer. It does not boost your reputation. It does not improve your sales.

Writing and publishing may be an oddball industry, but it's not actually a cutthroat competitive business like, say, rival snack chip manufacturers. If one author's novel sells well, that doesn't mean your book will sell less.

Readers are voracious, and most writers are readers. We want to cuddle up with a good book—something that we didn't write ourselves—as much as anyone else. In fact, the phenomenal success of *Harry Potter,* the *Twilight* books, or *The Hunger Games* created a large ripple effect. Readers picked up similar books, which helped the sales of other authors. Publishers and booksellers experienced higher profits. A rising tide lifts all boats.

Fan groups have endless debates nitpicking popular books, denigrating anything that has gotten too successful. But a professional author does not badmouth her peers. Writers who make snarky comments about *The Da Vinci Code, Fifty Shades of Grey, Harry Potter, Twilight,* even the film *Avatar*, just seem to have sour grapes.

Kevin once made a disparaging comment about *The Bridges of Madison County*—a phenomenally bestselling novel that he imagined to be a lightweight, sappy romance (without having read it). Rebecca scolded him. "Instead of criticizing, read the book and figure out *why* it touched so many people, then see what you can learn from that."

At the time *Bridges* had been on the major bestseller lists for countless weeks. The author, Robert James Waller, had obviously done something right, tapped into some particular need to attract such a flood of readers. Better to learn from that phenomenal success than to mock levels of sales that every writer dreams of. So, Kevin and Rebecca both read the book and analyzed what the author had done right and why it was such a breakout. Now we try to read every mammoth blockbuster to understand what popular nerve it touched and to see what we can learn from it to make our books better.

Cheer the fact that one of your colleagues has broken through that very thick ceiling. We've had many writing students over the years, and we celebrate their successes, delighted when they achieve things that we haven't. Kevin often jokes that he hopes his writing students will become so wildly successful that one day they'll give him a glowing blurb on one of his novels.

And that has happened several times.

Show Gratitude

Just in case you need the reminder, *thank the people who help you.*

You *know* that a lot of people participated in the writing of your novel, whether they helped you in your research, proofread the manuscript, did some typing or photocopying for you, brainstormed with you, got you coffee, babysat your kids, or just inspired you.

Editors or publishers will often take their authors out for a nice dinner. Early on, Rebecca asked Kevin to send a Thank You card after each such meal. He was puzzled. "But editors always take authors out. They don't expect a Thank You card." Rebecca insisted (and she can be very insistent). After he sent the first such card, Kevin received a shocked and appreciative phone call from the editor, who said that in his entire career nobody had ever bothered to send him a Thank You.

That's the impression you want to make. And it's just plain courteous.

Rebecca

In graduate school, I wrote a play that was performed by me and my fellow students. Each one of us worked hard making the video; we stayed up all night finishing the project, filming, cutting the music, and so on. Our project got an A. After class, another group member and I met with my professor, who said, "Rebecca, I just knew your group would do the best job in the whole class." It felt great to be complimented and to have all my hard work recognized. I beamed and said, "Thank you."

Later, my classmate took me aside and asked, "Didn't any of the rest of us do anything? Did you make that film all by yourself?" I was stunned. In my excitement, I had accepted our professor's praise all by myself, without thinking to mention anyone else. Even though I wrote the script, starred in the video, and put in more hours than anybody else, I could not have done it without the rest of my group. I had hurt my friend and slighted my other classmates, brushing them aside. I was so proud of my work that it never occurred to me to give other people credit. It wouldn't have cost me a thing.

Wow. I was an idiot. I apologized.

I always remember that lesson.

A lot of people's effort goes into the work that you do. If you're a writer, you probably have friends, a spouse, children, or other family who are giving up a lot to make sure you can do your writing. Honor anyone who helps you along the way. Putting people in the acknowledgments of your book is free, so be liberal with your gratitude.

Again, there are no unimportant people. Be friendly and professional with everyone you deal with in the business, whether it's a low-level employee in the mail room or the head of the company. Always note the names of administrators, assistants, junior staff members. When you call your editor's office because you need something, the assistant will be more inclined to help if you're polite and respectful, and remember that person's name, rather than thinking of them as "Nobody, who is the assistant to Big Name."

We've seen many talented and ambitious people start out in the mail room, work their way up to Editorial Assistant, then Assistant Editor, then Editor, and even higher. You'll be glad you treated them well when they were still on the lower rungs of the corporate ladder.

O O O

Kevin's very first editor, who bought four novels from him at Signet Books, eventually moved over to Warner Books where he remembered Kevin and bought two more novels from him. Then he took a position at HarperCollins, where he offered Kevin three X-Files novels (a big break for him at the time), and later went on to join a large literary agency … where he is now Kevin's agent.

O O O

Every book has a set of Acknowledgments. Remember to show your appreciation for anyone who takes time to assist you, who offered to critique the manuscript, or who gave you technical advice, as well as your editor, your agent, your publisher, other authors who supported you, and of course your patient spouse, significant other, or cat. Show that you remember what they did for you (although pets don't generally read Acknowledgments).

Being nice doesn't cost anything, but it can buy a lot.

Part II

Dirty Secrets

Dirty Secret № 1

Sheer Writing Talent Will Not Guarantee Success

There are many aspects to a writing career that you learn along the way, but nobody teaches you. Sometimes they are hard lessons to learn. We call them "Dirty Secrets."

The first Dirty Secret that even brilliant writers have to face is that sheer writing talent will not guarantee success.

Of course, it doesn't hurt to be the most genius writer on the planet, a person whose literary work can wring out emotion like dirty water from a soaked dishrag. But mere brilliance with words is not *enough* to make you a successful career author.

We knew an extremely talented, ingenious writer who won the grand prize in a major writing contest. His work was quirky, fabulous, imaginative, breathtaking. His stories—whenever he got around to writing and finishing them—were received by readers with utter delight. But he had no discipline, rarely managed to complete a work, refused to do rewrites when an editor suggested them, treated deadlines the way a race car driver views the speed limit. As a consequence, despite his incredible writing ability, he had trouble getting work, and soon vanished from the field.

Editors and publishers are running a *business*. They have customers to please, slots to fill, a schedule to keep. They would rather have a steady supply of really good novels that arrive on time and satisfy many readers, than the most breathtaking novel that never gets delivered and is never released. The mark of a professional writer, one who gets hired again and again, is a writer who produces consistently good work, delivers on time, is reliable in all aspects, and is pleasant and professional to work with.

When Kevin wrote his first several novels for Signet and Bantam Books, he turned in his manuscripts on time and did rewrites as requested, even though he had a full-time job. He caused his editors no stress, and they really appreciated a low-maintenance writer. He didn't know he was auditioning.

When the opportunity to write new *Star Wars* novels came up, his Bantam editor was asked to suggest authors who might be appropriate for the job. Entirely without Kevin's knowledge, the editor submitted his name to Lucasfilm, recommending him as reliable, flexible, and professional. Kevin got the job. He worked well with them, delivered his *Star Wars* projects on time and remained easy to work with. After he had proven himself, Lucasfilm offered him a lot more work. Eventually, he ended up doing 54 separate *Star Wars* projects.

Many other writers are more powerful literary magicians, but Kevin had the other qualities they were looking for—persistence, professionalism, and reliability. And that gives you an edge on plain old talent.

A Chinese proverb says "Persistence can grind an iron beam down to a needle." Calvin Coolidge said, "Nothing in the world can take the place of Persistence. Talent will not; nothing is more common than unsuccessful men with talent. Genius will not; unrewarded genius is almost a proverb. Education will not; the world is full of educated derelicts. Persistence and Determination alone, are omnipotent. The slogan PRESS ON has solved and will always solve the problems of the human race."

Persistence, persistence, persistence. As we will discuss below, dogged persistence and the refusal to give up will open doors and help you overcome the barriers set up against new writers where even the most brilliant prose isn't enough. Instead of a battering ram, it's like a steady drip of water eroding a stone wall. But you will get through.

DIRTY SECRET № 2

Personal Connections Really Can Help

It's a dirty secret that if you know the right people, you might get a faster response or a more favorable read. Having a personal connection with someone on the editorial staff or inside the publishing house could give you a leg up over a completely unknown new writer from outer East Podunk. That's a fact of life.

When an editor is staring at a pile of unsolicited manuscripts, story after story by unrecognizable names, a familiar name naturally draws special attention. If you have met the editor in person, even more so. In the sea of submissions, if an editor has a face to put with a name, it works to your advantage—unless you've made a negative first impression. (If necessary, review "Don't Be a Jerk," above.)

How do you make that personal connection if you're a newbie nobody?

One option is to go to writer's gatherings or conventions, which are often crowded with editors, publishers, agents, and fellow professionals—as well as your potential readers. This is your chance to meet them all. Make friends, and make connections.

Kevin has edited more than a dozen anthologies, and most of the contributors are drawn from his peers, friends, writing students, and ambitious new authors he's met in person. In addition to the usual social activity of hanging out with other writers, Kevin keeps an eye open for people he might like to work with, as well as noting the "never in a million years" writers. (Note, that goes for established pros as well as amateurs!) In an emergency, under a tight deadline, he can count on his circle of close writer friends to deliver a last-minute story to fill a gap.

When editing his first *Star Wars* anthology, *Tales from the Mos Eisley Cantina,* Kevin invited Dave Wolverton as one of the established professional contributors. The anthology was a collection of stories about the interesting characters in the famous *Star Wars* cantina scene, and he assigned a specific character to each writer. At the time, Dave was particularly impressed with one of his writing students who had a couple of publication credits and had just won a major writing contest. Dave suggested that the writer send samples to Kevin to see if there might be a spot for him in the book.

Now, this was a big-ticket anthology, and Kevin had all the important slots already assigned. He didn't want word to get around that he was open to random submissions, which would then flood his mailbox. But he read the samples from this new writer, and he liked the writing a lot. He decided to take a chance, chose an unimportant bit character in the background of the Cantina scene, and contacted the new writer. "I'll let you write a story on spec for the anthology. It's not an important character, so if your story isn't good enough, I can still leave it out. Your challenge is to write the absolute best story I have in the anthology. That's the way you'll get in."

The writer took the challenge—and sure enough he did turn in Kevin's favorite story in the entire book.

O O O

In order to make personal connections, meet people in all areas of your profession. You don't always know which way a business deal will go. We know novel writers, comic book writers, Hollywood script writers, game designers. We've become friends with actors, directors, producers, publishers, typesetters, people at all different levels of the book publishing and the entertainment industry. You never know what interesting connection is going to result in a new project.

When we go to conventions and conferences, we encourage our former writing students to say hi. If they do—thereby demonstrating that they have a professional mindset—we go out of our way to introduce them to editors, publishers, and other professionals. Making introductions is not just a lightweight favor, either—if we go to the trouble to introduce a newbie to an editor, we're putting *our own* reputations on the line. We're vouching for the new writer, and that editor pays attention. It's our way of paying forward.

Remember what you've read in this book: Present yourself well. Be polite, articulate, interesting, and considerate. Don't talk interminably about your novel; simply mention it, give a *two sentence description* (if you can't boil your novel down to a two-sentence teaser, then learn to do so), and mention that it is finished and ready to go—and it had better be ready to go. If the editor is at all interested, she will say, "Sure, send me the first fifty pages" or "Send me the whole manuscript."

Next step—and this is very important—ACTUALLY SEND WHATEVER THE EDITOR ASKED FOR.

When you return home, package up the manuscript (or send it by email, if that's what the editor prefers), and mail it with a polite letter to the editor.

Dear [*insert Editor's Name*],

"It was nice meeting you at [*insert Name of Event*]. As you requested, here is the novel we discussed. Thank you for agreeing to look at it."

Sincerely,

[*insert Your Name*]

Since you were polite and articulate, and demonstrated your proficiency with personal hygiene, the editor will remember who you are (in a good way). She will have a face to put with your name when the manuscript arrives with a pile of others. Because you've already broken the ice and made a good first impression, she will at least look at it.

From that point, it's your job as a writer to provide such a compelling manuscript that the editor will want to buy.

DIRTY SECRET №3

"Overnight Successes" Usually Aren't

Big celebrities who suddenly appear on your radar usually got there after years and years of hard work. It can take decades to achieve "overnight success."

Some outsiders have remarked on Kevin's "lucky breaks," believing that he became an "overnight success" as soon as he started writing *Star Wars* novels. But he had been writing—steadily—since he was eight years old. He submitted his first story for publication at age twelve. He got published at age fifteen, got paid for his first story at sixteen. He sold his first novel when he was 25. Seven years and ten books later, he had his first national bestseller—at age 32, twenty years after he sent out his first story for publication. Since most people never heard of him until after his first bestseller, many considered him an "overnight success," a young upstart who had no business hitting the *New York Times* bestseller list, because they thought he hadn't worked for it. It must have been a stroke of luck. But it was two decades in the making.

Dean Koontz had dozens of novels written before one hit the bestseller list. He used five or six different pseudonyms, plugging away at writing on book after book. Fortunately, the book that launched him as a superstar—*Whispers*—was published under his own name. Few readers noticed his name until one book became a major bestseller, but he had been publishing long before that.

Look at the example of actress Jennifer Love Hewitt. She first began performing on stage at the age of three. When she was ten years old, she wanted so much to become an actress that she convinced her mother to move to Hollywood from Texas. Her mother, a single mom, agreed to get a job in LA and support her daughter for one year, to see if she could get her big break. So they moved to California. Jennifer had one year.

She got some parts in commercials, then on the Disney Channel series *Kids Incorporated,* and on a kids' exercise video. She kept working at it. She didn't get a big break, but she had her foot in the door. In the interim she landed small roles in numerous plays, movies, working her way up with mostly bit parts. She finally hit it big in the TV show *Party of Five*, then the film *I Know What You Did Last Summer*, then *Ghost Whisperer, Law and Order, Criminal Minds*, and many other appearances.

When she started to appear prominently, people called Jennifer Love Hewitt another overnight success, without realizing that she had been working at her career for more than a dozen years before she achieved stardom. This did not just "happen."

Same with the singer and actress Brandy. She started singing and performing on stage when she was five years old. She rose to success in music at age fifteen, and became a TV star a few years later. She had been working at her career for more than ten years. Also not an overnight success.

Congratulations if phenomenal popularity lands in your lap with little or no effort on your part. But a genuine "overnight success"—somebody who instantly becomes a star without having to work their way up—is often just a flash in the pan.

The people with staying power have usually been working for decades to get where they are.

Dirty Secret No 4

Don't Let Writing Classes or Critique Groups Take the Place of Writing

A writing class is not a magic key to a successful writing career. Ask professional authors, especially bestselling authors, how many of them have advanced degrees in creative writing. You may find a few, but not many.

Of course, it's good to have a literary background to understand plot structures and characters, how fiction works. You do have to be facile with grammar, exposition, dialogue. But taking *only* English courses is like an aspiring master chef collecting a shelf full of cookbooks, without ever bothering to acquire pans, bowls, utensils, or even ingredients to cook with. Writing classes do a good job of teaching *part* of the writing process. Learn from them, but don't obsess on them.

Kevin has a degree in physics and astronomy, with a minor in Russian history. Rebecca has a Master's in Business Administration.

O O O

Kevin

At the University of Wisconsin, Madison, where I went to college, I applied for, and was accepted into, an exclusive "advanced fiction writing workshop," the crème de la crème of the university's writing courses. Many aspiring writers applied, but few were accepted into the elite class.

On the first day of the workshop, I learned to my surprise that the professor who would teach us how to become successful authors had published only a piece of poetry, in a no-pay literary magazine. That was his lone credential. He had never managed to publish a novel or a professional story of his own. At the time, as a sophomore in college, I already had more than a dozen short stories and articles published, and I was editing a completed novel. Hmmm, what made this guy such an expert?

When I asked whether he would be teaching the workshop students about the marketplace, how to deal with editors, how to submit to magazines and book publishers, the professor lifted his nose. "We don't teach that sort of thing here."

Almost weekly, I would come into class announcing a new sale or a story publication, which caused the one-poem professor a great deal of consternation. (He did give me a good grade, though.)

O O O

Also while in college, Kevin fell in with a writer's group that met on campus every Thursday afternoon (many of them from the advanced fiction writing workshop mentioned above). He thought that hanging around with other authors would be a great way to get inspiration and make connections.

This group of aspiring writers would sit in a local coffee house all afternoon, through dinner, and far into the night, sipping cappuccino or mineral water as they talked about the great novels they would publish someday. But hour after hour, they bemoaned the fact that they never had enough time to write.

Kevin discovered that if he just stopped going to their kaffeeklatsch and spent those hours writing instead, he could be amazingly productive. He devoted his time to writing instead of talking about writing.

Writing critique groups can also be useful. A cooperative batch of test readers can help you catch mistakes or inconsistencies. You get a trial run, to see how people react to your story, learn if they understand your plot twist or if they guess the solution to your mystery, if they laugh or cry when they're supposed to. Other critiquers might point out flaws in pacing, internal contradictions, even grammar or spelling mistakes.

Listen to the comments of a critique group, but don't be paralyzed by them. (See the appendix to this book, Consider the Source.) A group of untried and unproven writers does not necessarily yield infallible advice. Sometimes they are just wrong. Occasionally they carry personal baggage or begrudge other writers their achievements, especially if one member of the group begins to succeed when the others don't.

Kevin's early critique group grumbled about one of his novels with Doug Beason, *Assemblers of Infinity*, but their comments didn't ring true to him, and he published the manuscript in its original form. *Assemblers of Infinity* was serialized in the largest science fiction magazine, then published by Bantam Books, and was nominated for the Nebula Award, science fiction's highest honor. In the end, it's the opinion of the professional (paying) editor that really counts.

Dirty Secret № 5

The Wrong Agent Can Be Worse Than No Agent at All

Few subjects cause more angst among newbie authors than finding an agent. People beg us for advice and recommendations on agents, often before they've even written their first novel. That's planning too far ahead.

Sure, an agent can open doors for you in certain publishing companies. But many publishers will read unsolicited manuscripts, and if they do make an offer, *then* you can get an agent or a publishing lawyer before you sign a contract. If you don't have any credentials, however, how do you expect to land a big name, powerful agent? It's the old Catch-22. If you have minimal credits and connections, you'll get only a low-tier agent, who won't have much clout to open doors for you.

In particular, be leery of agents who advertise in writer's magazines or on discussion boards. Every worthwhile agent we know has a full stable of writers, and none of them feels the need to advertise for unproven neophyte authors in hopes of finding the next great literary master.

O O O

Kevin

When I was in high school, sending out my first short stories and working on book one of an epic fantasy trilogy (as everybody did in those days), I set out to get an agent. I discovered a classified ad in the back of Writer's Digest *magazine. A "respected literary agency" was looking for new clients. Oh, boy! So I wrote to the PO Box in the ad and told the agent about my education, my work up to that point, and my career plans, and I gave her a synopsis of my epic fantasy.*

I received an enthusiastic letter back, promising that she would read my novel manuscript and (I'm not kidding) pointing out that since Star Wars was such a hit movie, she was sure she could sell "that kind of thing."

And, by the way, there was also a fifty dollar reading fee.

I was just sixteen years old with big ambitions, and it was tough to come up with fifty dollars, but this was my future writing career. I wanted to be a professional writer, so I made the investment, sent her my novel, which (surprise!)

she loved and was sure she could sell. She told me to send more of my work.

So, for the next year, I wrote story after story and sent every single one of them to her so she could place them in magazines. It was like throwing them down a black hole. When I grew impatient for some feedback from editors, to see some acceptances and contracts, she suddenly answered with the wonderful news that "one of the Lippincott magazines" had accepted two of my stories! She named the magazines. I had never heard of them, nor could I find them on the newsstand, but Lippincott was a name to conjure with in the publishing industry, so it had to be real, right?

I signed the contracts. I was walking on air. I was going to be a published writer! They even promised to pay me five cents a word, a princely sum, which would more than pay off the fifty dollars I had sent the agent to read my novel. I was insufferably pleased with myself for quite some time.

Then the other shoe dropped.

The agent wrote that the Lippincott magazines were upgrading their technology and purchasing an expensive new phototypesetting system. Because of their investment, they were asking all their authors to share the cost of producing their work. They wanted me to invest a hundred dollars for my stories to be typeset and then published.

Warning bells should have gone off, but I was naïve, optimistic (and a "soon to be a published author").

By happy coincidence, however, in my high school—I was a senior by then—I was taking a graphic arts class, and our school had just acquired the very same phototypesetting machine the Lippincott magazines used. I asked my teacher, and he graciously granted me permission to stay after school and typeset my own stories, according to the magazine specs. I wrote my agent the good news that I wouldn't need to spend the one hundred dollars because I could provide exactly the finished copy they wanted, and I asked for their detailed specs.

She wrote back a curt letter a week later, saying that, nevermind, the magazine wouldn't need authors to pay for the typesetting after all.

Months of silence followed, despite my inquiries. Then I received a notice from the FBI saying that my agent had been arrested and charged with mail fraud. During the investigation, they returned all my manuscripts to me, my thick fantasy novel and a dozen short stories—all still in their original envelopes.

She had never submitted them anywhere.

By foolish luck, I had lost only the initial fifty dollars, so all in all, it was a relatively inexpensive lesson to learn. But I also lost a year and a half of time. I could have been submitting those stories and that novel to real markets rather than having them sit in a drawer in a fraudulent agent's office.

I didn't attempt to get an agent again until I had a handful of real professional publication credits from major magazines. And the next time I searched for an agent, I checked him out, talked to some of his clients, and verified the sales he had made, before I agreed to sign on. He went on to sell many books for me.

Dirty Secret №6

Advertising Is Expensive. Publicity Is Cheap.

Just because your book is published, doesn't mean anyone will buy it. How do you get the word out?

Many authors—indie authors, especially—go to great lengths to promote their new book: t-shirts, key chains, bookmarks, posters, imprinted chocolate bars. They pay for ads in magazines, do mass mailings of postcards, go on blog tours, or even actual book tours from city to city (all on their own dime).

That can add up to a lot of money, often much more than you can ever hope to make from sales of your book. Sometimes that works; more often it doesn't. And even when your promotional efforts do catch on, you might not see any concrete results until four or more books later. Publicity is rarely instantaneous, like hitting the jackpot on a lottery ticket. It's more like droplets of water falling onto a stone *drip, drip, drip, drip*, taking their effect over the course of many years.

Hoping to get ahead, some authors hire expensive publicists, or contract with marketing agencies or book-promotional services. But it's not easy to get serious media coverage for any novel, much less an indie published novel by an unknown writer.

When Brian Herbert and Kevin sold their first major *Dune* contract, they believed they had something newsworthy. The new trilogy was the largest single science fiction contract in publishing history: these were the first *Dune* novels to be published in more than a decade. Their trilogy was a prequel to the best-selling science fiction novel of all time! How could media outlets not fall all over themselves to cover the story?

The two were talked into spending $75,000 out of pocket on a publicist who was sure to take the entertainment world by storm with all the coverage she promised to get. Slam dunk.

Over several months, though, she managed to get only a single two-line mention in one gossip column in one New York newspaper. Nothing else. Nada. For $75,000.

We've since worked with many other publicists, hoping we didn't just get the lone bad apple. Some of them were from a major publisher's publicity department, others were freelancers. Two of them were fantastic, while the rest were … less so. Paying for a marketing blitz, or hiring an expensive publicist, is probably not the wisest investment. Advertising is expensive.

Publicity, however, is cheap. If you can get your book covered in a local newspaper or trade magazine, or if you can book yourself on a local radio station, find book signing opportunities at local stores, get mentioned on large blog sites, do a library talk—those are free. If you have a newsworthy hook, if something about your novel makes you an expert in a particular field, then pitch that to media outlets. If you have done something for a prominent charity, you can get coverage for that and also mention your book.

Social media is also free, although it takes time and a lot of energy. You can build your fan base, gather like-minded people around you, keep a mailing list, entertain them, but don't incessantly plug your novel. The main thing your followers will want is content, not advertisements.

The most important investment of time for a professional writer—a writer who intends to have a long-term career—is to *write the next book* and build a fan base that way.

PART III

THE BUSINESS MINDSET

Get to Know Your Business

No one cares as much about your writing career as you do. No one. Not your agent, not your editor, not your accountant, not your author buddies. *You* have to pay attention. *You* have to keep track of your business, and *you* have to learn how the business works.

Learn about writing, develop your craft, observe other writers. Study the expectations of whatever genre you're working in. Improve your prose, your characterization, your setting. Be the best writer you can possibly be.

But that's just the first step.

Publishing is a complicated and even somewhat irrational business model, and the publishing world is currently undergoing great upheavals. Even well-informed experts in the field can barely stay on top of all the changes. More than ever, you have to keep track of the business of publishing and bookselling.

Don't count on someone else to do it for you.

Gone are the days when a writer can live like a hermit in a cabin, turn in a finished novel, and expect the publisher's team to take care of everything else. Be proactive and get involved in your own career. Learn about the industry. Read trade magazines or blogs such as *Publishers Weekly* or *Publishers Lunch*. Follow the trends in the marketplace, keep an eye on changes in technology and distribution, and understand how bookselling works.

Why does one book get displayed prominently in the window while another is shelved spine out? What happens to books that can't be sold and have to be returned? Why does Amazon feature one title prominently on their homepage, while similar books never appear on your screen? How does your novel get selected as the other title on "if you liked that book, you might also enjoy this one" recommendations?

Answering those questions would take another entire book. It's a long process, and you need to do your homework. Study the field. Become a professional with a business mindset.

O O O

Keep track of your personal business as well, which includes your contracts, receipts, accounts receivable, future tax obligations. Learn what qualifies as a writing expense and what doesn't. Keep track of your mileage when you drive to a book signing, your professional development expenses at writers' conferences, your postage, your printer toner and paper, your web design fees, your travel to conventions where you talk about your novel.

Tax laws are intricate and specific to your location and your individual situation, and we are not going to advise you on those matters. Talk to your accountant, learn what you can and can't write off, and understand how you need to file your taxes.

You are running a *small business.* Small businesses keep track of their operating expenses. Small businesses do their paperwork. They track bills paid and payments received. As you begin selling your work and the euphoria is over, you need to keep track of which publishers owe you money and when it is due (and when it is late), when a story or a book is set to be released, and whether or not you've received your contributor's copies.

New authors may be astonished. How could you ever lose track of whether you've been paid for a story or book? Or whether you've received a published copy? Domestic publishers can run months behind in paying. Foreign publishers are notoriously slow in issuing contracts and in making their (usually modest) payments.

Foreign contracts often have a specific term, which expires after a set amount of time. If a book is translated into, say, Bulgarian, the publisher has the right to sell that book for a certain number of years, after which the contract terminates. The Bulgarian publisher isn't going to go out of their way to tell you the term has expired and that you are free to resell those rights. Keep track of when that time expires so you can renew the contract or sell the rights elsewhere.

Read your contracts and know what you're agreeing to. (And once you've agreed to the terms, don't whine about it afterward if you decide you don't like something.)

Contracts are negotiable. Publishers will ask for everything they could possibly want, hoping to get great terms. You don't have to agree to everything. Some terms are firm, but publishers will often budge on certain provisions, such as the number of author copies you receive or the length of time before you can reprint a story. They may ask for worldwide rights, but will accept US/Canada rights only (allowing you to sell the non-US rights elsewhere).

You don't know unless you ask.

Authors will complain about draconian terms and cutthroat publishers, when they simply didn't read or negotiate their contracts. And if you don't read your contracts before signing them, then a publisher will (legitimately) turn a deaf ear to your complaints afterward.

O O O

Kevin

For one of my anthologies, I asked authors to write stories based on a popular media franchise. They agreed to the basic terms, the pay rate, and the deadline, after which they wrote and delivered their stories.

Then the licensor presented me with the contract I had to send them, which included one appalling provision I had never seen before. When writing work-for-hire fiction, it's understood that the authors have to make certain sacrifices and abide by certain restrictions, but when I saw one particular clause the licensor wanted me to include, I balked. I had never seen such terrible terms before! It was non-standard and unnecessarily ruthless. As editor, I argued with the licensor, saying, "I can't have my authors sign that clause! It's not part of the generally accepted terms they understood when they agreed to write a story for me."

After several back and forth conversations, the licensor compromised. Their legal department insisted that the clause needed to be in the boilerplate contract, but any author who objected to that paragraph was allowed to cross it out. That seemed a good enough solution to me, so I sent out the contracts.

Shortly thereafter, I received angry phone calls from fifteen of the sixteen contributors, outraged at the terms. After I calmed them, I told them to strike the clause, and we were fine. I heard nothing from the sixteenth author, though—and a few days later I received his signed contract back in the mail.

Being a nice editor, I contacted him. "So ... I received your signed contract."

"Yes," he said cheerily. "I got it, signed it, and sent it right back."

I frowned. "And you were okay with the terms in it?"

He laughed. "I never read those things. I just sign them and send them off."

At which point, I had done as much of a good deed as I could justify. We went on to publish the anthology.

Learn to Accept Rejection

Rejection is part of the business. Think of it like riding a bicycle: When you fall down, you get back up and try again. If you don't submit your work for publication, you will never be published. And when you *do* submit, you are going to be rejected. Guaranteed. No one is so brilliant as to hit every editor's tastes every time. Don't take it personally, but learn from any comments the editor might make.

Editors are business people with a job to do and a magazine or a book line to run. They make decisions based on their company's criteria, the mission of their publication, the interests of their readership.

An editor might turn down your submission because the story is no good or your writing is terrible, but those aren't the only potential reasons. It's also possible that the publishing house had just purchased a piece along similar lines, or maybe your upbeat manuscript just doesn't fit with the somber tone the editor wants for the magazine.

There may be even more subtle reasons for rejection, things few writers can prepare against. Your sympathetic main character might have the same name as the editor's reviled ex-boyfriend. The politics of the story could be against the editor's personal philosophy. The subject could be something that simply pushes the editor's hot buttons.

One of our author friends wrote a science fiction story about thrill seekers who record their near-death experiences, which they then sell for popular entertainment. Though the editor had requested the story from him, she rejected it, explaining that she herself had had a dramatic near-death experience, and she simply couldn't bear to read a story on the subject.

When going through a stack of manuscripts, editors are not looking for reasons to keep reading—they're looking for any possible reason to *stop.* Don't give them that reason. If sloppy prose, or a ridiculous plot twist, or an expository lump, or unbelievable dialogue knocks the editor out of the story, she'll be relieved to toss the manuscript aside and pick up the next one in the stack.

Diana Gill, Executive Editor at Ace and Roc Books, says, "I'm being paid to read these submissions. If I'm being *paid* and I can't get through a manuscript, how can I expect readers to *pay* to read it?"

Always start at the top. When you've finished polishing a story and are ready to market it, send it to the biggest, highest-paying market that is appropriate. Sure, the competition will be more fierce, but what if your story really *is* that good? Don't you want it to be in the most impressive publication? Don't you want the bigger paycheck? The widest possible audience?

Don't take the easy way out. Sure, if you send your story to a small magazine or website, your chances of acceptance might be greater—but what if your work could have won an award, or been chosen for the Year's Best anthology if it had been seen in the larger market? Try the top publication first, then the next one, then the next one, and work your way down.

Submit to the *proper market*, don't just mail your work willy-nilly like a blindfolded man throwing darts at a board. Delivering what the editor is looking for takes due diligence on your part. Don't send something inappropriate "just in case." A mystery magazine editor doesn't want to see a hard science fiction novelette. A women's magazine doesn't want the story of a barbarian swordsman. A science fiction magazine doesn't want to read a teen romance story.

There are fewer surefire ways to annoy an editor than to intentionally waste his or her time.

O O O

Kevin

My Blood Lite *anthologies had a simple, clear theme: horror stories with humor. Any type of horror, dark fantasy, or thriller, so long as it was funny. I didn't think there was anything too complicated about that.*

One story came in about a serial killer who kidnapped, raped, and murdered college women. It was disturbing, but well written, so I kept going, waiting for the big laugh. The story was grim, unsettling, violent … and as I neared the end I couldn't imagine what the punchline would be. On the last page, the killer dispatched one victim and captured another to repeat the cycle all over again. The end.

I was shocked. In what conceivable universe did the author think that story would be appropriate for Blood Lite*? When I wrote my rejection letter, I asked the author what he felt was funny in the manuscript? Where was the punchline? Why would he think I might want to include this particular story in* Blood Lite*? He responded, "Oh, the story wasn't supposed to be funny, but it was the only manuscript I had ready, so I thought I'd give it a try. Why not?"*

That made me really angry. I had a large stack of manuscripts to read, and I'd just spent half an hour reading a story that I could never, ever have accepted for a humorous horror anthology—and the author knew it before he submitted the manuscript. He had wasted my time!

One thing I did remember was the author's name, and he will automatically be on my poop list if I receive a submission from him again.

Kevin started submitting stories to magazines when he was twelve years old. Granted, at the time his writing was execrable, but he was determined to be a writer. So he kept writing and kept sending stories out, undeterred by the constant stream of rejections he received. Having read some of those early efforts, Rebecca has told him that if she'd known him back then, she would have encouraged him to find another line of work....

But Kevin was stubborn, kept mailing out story after story, writing new pieces while resubmitting the old ones to market after market (always starting at the top), and over the course of time, he got better. He collected eighty rejection slips before his first story was ever published (in a Wisconsin high school student-writings magazine, which paid only in contributor's copies). He continued submitting, and a year later he actually sold a story—for $12.50. After that, he was a "published author" who had been paid for his work.

Persistence. Persistence. Persistence.

He has since racked up over seven hundred rejection slips, enough to earn him a genuine trophy: a golden statuette on a marble block, with an engraved placard that names him "The Writer with No Future," because he could produce more rejection slips *by weight* than any other writer at an entire conference. He still proudly displays the trophy in a place of honor—atop the toilet tank in the bathroom of his office.

It's a testament to persistence and improvement.

Many of our writing students tell us they are discouraged and ready to give up after fifteen or twenty rejections. But if Kevin had given up at twenty or fifty or seventy, he would never have been published anywhere. That was 23 million copies ago. Good thing he stuck with it.

Rebecca didn't have quite the same mindset at first, though.

O O O

Rebecca

My father was an English teacher, and I knew language, grammar, punctuation, and the components of a good story. I convinced myself that I could write circles around most of the people I'd read in print. Once I submitted a manuscript, I was certain the editor would read my work, fall to her knees, and weep with joy at having discovered a new literary light. She would call me and beg to publish everything I wrote from then on.

So, encouraged by Kevin, I finally sent a story to a fantasy magazine, expecting that not only would it be accepted, it would be the cover story. I'd win awards and be hailed as the next great genius.

The manuscript came back in the mail with a two-page personal rejection letter explaining why the story didn't work. How could that be? And the editor was a friend of ours, too!

I was crushed. I was a failure. How could I ever look our editor friend in the eye again for having submitted an unacceptable piece of fiction? I was dejected.

I whined.

And Kevin, with an uncharacteristic lack of support—and many hundreds of rejection slips of his own—told me to suck it up and send out the story again.

I had to learn not to take rejection personally. I wrote more stories, submitted them again—and yes, I did eventually get published.

Rejections are a part of your job, not a referendum on your talent or your career.

We were recently instructors at a pro-level anthology workshop, along with four other established editors. Nearly fifty students submitted stories to six different themed anthologies, and the whole panel of pro editors discussed the manuscripts in front of the students, explaining whether or not we would buy each submission.

As the stories were discussed, the students listened in amazement as the six editors gave wildly different reactions to the same manuscript. One editor absolutely loved a story, while another hated it, and others were indifferent. Same story, different editors, entirely different results.

You can do your best to study the market, and also to write your best story, but you can't predict whether or not an editor will reject it.

So write another one and submit it again. And again.

Don't Quit Your Day Job

Many of us dream about becoming full-time writers, but it doesn't always work out that way, even for authors who are quite successful. Don't quit your day job.

Obviously, that's not a hard-and-fast rule. After all, we are both full-time writers—that's how we pay the bills. But you'd be taking a gigantic risk, especially in the current tumultuous state of the publishing industry. Be very, very cautious before abandoning a regular paycheck, with benefits, for the capricious and unpredictable livelihood of a freelancer.

Once, at a science fiction convention, Kevin listened as a fellow panelist proudly announced that he had sold his first short story to *Analog* magazine for $350. Since he now had a professional sale in a major SF magazine, he had quit his well-paying and secure civil-service job so he could become a full-time writer.

We never heard from him again.

Just because you can sell a story or a book today doesn't mean you'll be able to sell the next one. Reader tastes change. Editors change. Publishers go out of business. Many writers can't work under a deadline, or they can't sell a project based on a premise and an outline.

Even when you have a signed contract, *publishers don't always pay on time.* But your electric bill needs to be paid on time. Your rent or mortgage needs to be paid on time. You have to pay for food at the grocery store when you purchase it, not sometime later whenever the advance check comes in. Even if you have a contract guaranteeing you payment "on publication" of your book, and even though the publisher knows *to the day*—many months in advance—when your book will be released, the payment will usually be late. Few publishers will actually cut a check and have it in your mailbox on or before the day of publication.

And you can't count on earning royalties either. Royalties are based on sales, which you can't predict, and large publishers have complex and incomprehensible algorithms in the way they report sales and royalties. They also keep large chunks of your money as a "reserve against returns," withholding payment just in case a bookstore returns books that were shipped long before.

In a situation like that, it's very hard to budget and do financial planning.

We don't get paid vacation; if we take a day off and don't do any writing, we don't make any income that day.

We don't get sick leave. If we're too ill to write, we don't make any income that day. And we have to pay for our health insurance and medical expenses out of pocket.

We don't have any retirement plan, except for the accounts we set up ourselves. If a publisher decides not to buy our next novel and we can't get any work, we do not collect unemployment.

Try applying for a mortgage by telling the banker that you're an author and hope to make a living at it someday. When we bought our first house, even though we had saved a substantial down payment and Kevin had six bestsellers under his belt and multiple books under contract, the lending agency requested that we get a letter from his publisher guaranteeing they would buy the next twelve books Kevin wrote. (No, that didn't happen!)

Kevin didn't actually quit his day job until he had seven *New York Times* bestsellers, and we had set aside an entire year's worth of expenses in a savings account. Even then, Rebecca continued working for several more years so that we could keep our benefits.

On the other hand, if you have a day job, you receive a regular, predictable check. You get vacation, sick leave, retirement. You get health benefits. You have stability.

Think carefully before you give up job security.

Build and Maintain Your Reputation

In addition to talent and imagination, one of a writer's greatest assets is her reputation. Do you want to be known as a difficult person to deal with? An unpleasant writer in social situations? One who is perennially late? One who can't manage money and is constantly nagging for checks that aren't even due? A bombastic rabble-rouser who picks fights online? A curmudgeon who is rude to his fans?

Or are you someone who is reliable? Who delivers acceptable work on time. Who is polite and businesslike. Who appreciates fans and treats them well. *That's the reputation you want.*

Editors and publishers have enough variables to consider in the constantly changing publishing business without adding the difficulty of a temperamental prima-donna writer. They aren't looking for high-maintenance authors.

Keep track of your own credits. Talk up what's good and unique about yourself and use it in your writing, your art, or your business career. If you have special talents, if you've immersed yourself in other cultures, if you've accomplished something remarkable, use that. If you've won awards, share that with people.

You don't have to do it in a boastful way, and you certainly don't want to imply that you are better than the person you are talking to, but there is nothing wrong with stating good facts about yourself.

Don't snivel and talk yourself down, either. Everybody has failed somewhere. Everybody has goofed up. Everybody has thought something was going to take off but it fizzled. Those aren't the things to focus on. Pick yourself up after your mistakes and move ahead. Concentrate on the things that went right.

If an interviewer or a fan or a friend brings up a failure, you don't need to deny it—especially if it's true. Focus on what was positive about the experience, what you learned from it.

Keep track of your statistics and reviews. How many books (or stories or articles) have you written? How many books do you have in print (or ebooks sold)? Have you hit any bestseller lists? Have you won awards? Has your work been translated into other languages? Did a reviewer call you "the next Robert Heinlein"?

These are all vital statistics for the future of your career. Put all of that information in a file and keep it up to date. Your agent won't keep track of it. Agents have many clients to serve, each with countless bits of information to maintain. You may also switch agents at some point. Your publisher or editor or publicist will not keep track. You will probably work for a variety of publishers in your career. Only you are familiar with all of your information.

Save every positive review of your work from newspapers, magazines, professional review sites, etc. (but not casual reviews, like those posted on Amazon.com or on your blog or written for you by your friends). Take special note of general reviews of your writing, rather than just the ones that talk about a specific book or story. Nonspecific quotes can be used again and again. For example, if a review says, "*Thornwoggle* was a magical book," you can only use that quote when referring to the book *Thornwoggle*. But if a review says you are "the most magical writer to come along since J.K. Rowling," you can quote that review on any of your writing projects. Treasure those quotes, and don't lose them.

You, and only you, have responsibility for creating and maintaining your reputation.

O O O

At Disney World, parts of the Magic Kingdom are public (for guests) and parts are private (for employees only). As soon as employees walk through a door to the public side, they are officially "on stage," and as soon as they walk back behind the door they are "backstage." Employees are referred to as Cast Members to remind them that every moment at Disney World they are playing a part and representing Disney World.

This is a good lesson for all professionals to remember: any time you're with people, you are in public. You are "on stage."

When you speak at a conference, you don't suddenly disappear once you leave the microphone. Readers will still know who you are. They'll hear you if you badmouth fans or other writers or convention staff; private conversations get relayed (and often exaggerated). To avoid this problem, it's simplest to follow the "Thumper Rule" from the Walt Disney movie *Bambi*: "If you can't say somthin' nice, don't say nothin' at all."

Kevin learned early on by watching one of his mentors and writer friends, bestselling fantasy author Terry Brooks. Even when faced with a long line of fans for a signing that went on for hours, where people kept asking the same question again and again, Terry was as gracious and warm to his fans as anyone could possibly want. He stayed the extra time until the line was gone and everyone's books were signed. He looked each person in the eye, showing that he was paying attention to them and that he genuinely appreciated that they bought and read his books.

Conversely, when Brian Herbert and Kevin were on tour for one of their bestselling Dune novels, they followed a day behind another author on the book-signing circuit. Kevin and Brian always arrive at their signings on time. They meet the bookstore staff. They shake the hands of the fans, give a friendly talk, and answer questions. Before they leave, they sign the store's leftover stock so that anyone who missed the signing can still pick up an autographed copy.

Night after night on that tour, bookstore owners would grouse about the previous author—a comedian who was decidedly not funny in person, habitually showed up late, was rude to the fans as well as the store staff, and insulted people who bought the book. The publisher received so many complaints about this bad behavior that they pulled the author halfway through the tour, since the personal appearances were causing more harm than good.

O O O

Kevin

When I was a young fan going to conventions, I met one of my favorite authors. I carried a first edition of his most famous novel, one I had enjoyed and told many other readers about. I wanted to get it autographed, so I could proudly display it on my shelf. Spotting the author having coffee in between panels, I politely went up to him, showed off the first edition, told him how much I loved his book, and asked for his autograph. He snapped, "Go away, I'm not signing books now," and ignored me.

It would have taken him a few seconds to make me an extremely happy fan. But instead, I felt slapped down. And

I've never read another one of his novels since then.

Rebecca

I was in Germany teaching at an Army base, and we had very limited access to new books. Every month, though, a new Star Trek paperback would show up at the Stars and Stripes bookstore on base. I bought and read each one.

Years later, I was delighted to meet the author of one of those Star Trek novels that had gotten me through those days in Germany. I expressed how much I enjoyed the work, but instead of being gracious and accepting the compliment, the author grimaced. "Star Trek! Why does everybody always talk about my Star Trek book? I wish they'd read something else of mine. I've written a lot of books since then."

I never want to treat one of my fans like that, no matter which books of mine they've read.

On the other hand, when I met the wonderful Anne McCaffrey and asked for her autograph, she gave me a very apologetic look and explained that she was in a great deal of arthritis pain. She simply couldn't sign autographs that day, but she didn't like to disappoint fans, so she had prepared for this possibility. She reached into a handbag, brought out an autographed bookplate, and asked if I would accept that instead.

Now that's classy.

Take pride in all your work. If someone tells you that your writing touched them or gave them enjoyment, or that you are their (or their friend's) favorite author, do not act modest and brush off the compliment they just gave you. And don't say "That's not really my best work." When readers take time to express that your work meant something to them, always say thank you and accept the praise. You can also tell them about similar books you've written that they might enjoy.

Above all, be gracious.

You are responsible for your own professional image. You are in charge of feeding it, making sure it's healthy, and letting other people know who you are. You can take charge of it.

And when you choose people to represent you—your agents, for example—choose carefully, because they are an important key to your success. How they represent you needs to be in line with how you want to be represented. There have been some authors, actors, artists, and musicians who were represented by such hard-nosed or rude agents that people assumed that the person behind the agent was actually that way, as well.

One way to maintain your good reputation is to be who you are all the time. Don't be one way among your friends and then act in a completely different way when you're in public. Who you are is who you are, and the way you behave is the gold standard that backs it up.

Success Breeds Success

There's enough to go around.

Surround yourself with people who are actually doing what you want to do (rather than just talking about doing it). If you hang out with successful people in the field, some of that success might rub off. It's not just a halo effect—you'll be in the right place at the right time, and you'll observe the habits, activities and attitudes of other successful people. Something worked for them. Pay attention to what it was.

A professional writing career is a gigantic and complex puzzle with numerous moving parts. Different writers at any stage of development might understand various pieces. They'll have clues that you don't have, and vice versa. You can help one another. You can build a support group.

Colleagues who are constantly writing and sending out stories share a pool of energy, resources, and information. And you can pay them back and do your part. When you hear about an anthology invitation or some other writing project, you may have a chance to forward the news to a friend or even tell the editor, "I know somebody who writes exactly this type of thing. They would be perfect if there's a slot open."

We've always worked hard to help other writers, whether newbies or established pros. We expect and receive the same in return.

O O O

You will see this among actors or comedians, too—a group of famous, successful people actually grew up together and have been friends for years, even when they were unknowns. How did they all become successful together? That would seem statistically unlikely. It's because success breeds success. The people who are willing to work hard will help each other out along the way.

As a young writer, Kevin met and befriended other aspiring authors and kept in touch with them as their careers began to grow. At the time, none of them had any credits, just similar goals. And you probably know at least some of them now: David Farland, Kristine Kathryn Rusch, Dean Wesley Smith, Michael A. Stackpole, Nina Kiriki Hoffman, Robert J. Sawyer, and Jennifer Roberson.

We were all new writers, learning our craft and learning the business. We poured our hearts and our

energies into becoming writers. As a group of frie
we helped one another, passing along news and tips,
critiquing manuscripts, sharing assignments, making introductions.

This wasn't helping "the competition." It was building an alliance. By pooling our knowledge, we didn't make ourselves less likely to succeed. We didn't become negative competition for each other—we became each others' *secret weapon.*

In the years since we were all newbies together, members of our group have become national and international bestselling authors, winners of (or nominees for) almost every award in numerous genres—from the Writers of the Future Award, to the Hugo, Nebula, World Fantasy, Philip K. Dick, Bram Stoker, Shamus, Edgar, Pushcart, Endeavor, Sidewise, Scribe, Locus, Mythopoeic Society, Romantic Times Reviewers' Choice, and Theodore Sturgeon Awards (and probably many others). Some have become publishers themselves, movie producers, record producers, or game designers.

We have a business mindset—a *professional* mindset. We are all career oriented, goal oriented, and doing exactly what we want to do. By working together and supporting one another, one success bred another success and another.

Appendix

Consider the Source

Rebecca Moesta

From a Keynote Speech for Life, the Universe, and Everything Symposium

Brigham Young University

As I was preparing to give a talk for the attendees of this symposium, I found myself thinking, Why should someone want to hear me speak—or even take advice from me? And why should you listen to what I have to say? Then I thought, well, maybe I'd better start with an entirely separate speech called "Consider the Source," on how, or whether, to take advice from someone.

So before I even try to give you advice, I'm going to give you advice on taking advice.

I have a Master's in Business Administration, so I tend to approach things from a business point-of-view and try to analyze cost–benefit ratios and things like that. Let me start out by analyzing what makes advice worth taking—because sometimes free advice is worth as much as you paid for it.

We all want to learn from other people's mistakes and successes. We need to find a good source for advice, because if you reinvent the wheel, you may also be reinventing all of the mistakes that people made leading up to it. That will put you well behind where you want to be. Choose a role model or mentor, but choose wisely.

Consider the source.

It's not a good idea to take advice about success from people who aren't successful themselves. That may sound like an overly simplified statement, but I have made this mistake many times in my past, and I know many people who listen very seriously to people who are *not successful.*

If you want to be a successful writer or artist, take advice from somebody who is at a level higher than you have achieved. Don't choose someone at the same level as you, or even below your level.

I took creative writing when I was in college, and I had a professor who hated everything I wrote. Everything I did was wrong from this teacher's point of view. Wrong, wrong, wrong! I was crushed. Every time I listened to another student's story—a story so good that everybody in the class was saying "Wow!" before bursting into applause—the teacher absolutely ripped it to shreds, telling them they didn't know anything about writing.

It wasn't until about ten years later—a decade during which I did no writing whatsoever—that I realized the professor had published only one small book of poetry in his entire career. That was it. Just a couple hundred copies of a little chapbook, and he had been interviewed on one local radio station. Other than teaching some writing classes, that booklet was the sum total of his experience with writing. He had convinced me that I was a bad writer and that I could never become a writer. So I didn't pursue writing because I was afraid for many, many long years. I should never have listened to *his* advice.

You have to consider the source.

When choosing your mentor, look at whether that person is going where you want to go. One of Kevin's mentors was Dean Koontz. That's not to say Kevin camped out in front of Dean's house in Southern California and asked for daily snippets of wisdom. Kevin would talk with him a couple of times a year, and if we found ourselves in an unexpected situation—something we'd never done before—he might call to consult Dean about what he would do.

No matter how much you respect a person, make sure that they have some experience in the area in which they're giving advice. Choose somebody who has credibility. You may want to learn from me in the area of business—or maybe not—but I would suggest you don't ask my advice in the area of, say, flying an airplane. I've met some very interesting Catholic priests who have great insights on building a relationship with God, but I draw the line at having them tell me the ins-and-outs of raising children, because most of them have no practical experience in that area.

There are *Writer's Digest*–style books that will tell you how to write a bestselling novel, but pay attention to who wrote them. Has the author of that book actually *written* a bestselling novel? Use your logic filter. "Why should I listen to this person?"

Let's say you pick up a book called *Writing the Blockbuster Novel* by Al Zuckerman. You probably haven't heard of Al Zuckerman before, haven't seen his name on the cover of bestselling novels. Why should he be giving advice? But if you read the author bio, you'll discover that he was the agent to many major *New York Times* bestselling novelists, including Ken Follett and Eileen Goudge. In that case, I decided he *did* know enough about the subject and was qualified to write a book on it.

Unfortunately, there are a lot of other books of advice written by people who have had no success in the area in which they are promoting themselves as experts.

Aspiring writers often look to their writers' group for advice, and I will give you another big caveat. If the other writers in the critique group are not where you want to go—or on their way to where you want to go—maybe think twice about what they say. Put it through your logic filter and ask yourself, "Does it make sense? Do they know what they're talking about?" Don't just accept that if they're in a writing group they must know about writing.

Fellow professionals can be an excellent resource for advice. Again, choose from the people who are ahead of you in the area that you want to advance in. For example, if you want to go into comic writing, look for advice from a comic industry professional, but don't necessarily take advice from them on writing a novel. Or if you want to learn how to write a TV script, look to someone who has TV credentials.

There is also the matter of practicality. Kevin's parents were a big help here, even if he didn't want to hear it. He wanted to be creative, to be a writer; he imagined himself doing big things with lots of readers for his work. But his parents insisted that he should get a job that would pay his bills, that he needed to cover his living expenses, to keep him afloat while he established himself as a writer.

He was disappointed that they weren't more supportive, just embracing his dreams no matter what. In fact, they wanted him to succeed—but also to be practical. He did get a good job as a technical writer to support himself, and he kept that job for twelve years while he was building his novel-writing career until it would support him. That was being practical. His parents gave him the right advice.

A lot of people take advice from friends, family, parents, peers, but at the end of the day, *you* are the person who's going to have to follow the path that you have chosen to the end of your life, after everybody else fades away or loses touch. Choose a career you can feel passionate about, something you want to keep doing, a job that will hold your enthusiasm and give you satisfaction, probably for the rest of your life.

So, that is my advice on taking advice and being successful. And it's just advice, so don't just take my word on all of these things. Think about it and decide for yourself.

Acknowledgments

We're grateful to many people for their various contributions to this book, which has been a work in progress for more than two decades. Thanks to

- Writers of the Future, where we first started giving this talk, and the support of Tim Powers, David Farland, K.D. Wentworth, Nina Kiriki Hoffman, John Goodwin of Galaxy Press, Gunhild Jacobs and Joni Labaqui of Author Services, among many others at the Contest.
- Everyone at WordFire Press who helped make this book possible: Peter J. Wacks, Keith J. Olexa, Quincy J. Allen, Vivian Trask, Sam Knight, Diane Jones, and David Boop.
- Terry Brooks for setting a stellar example of professionalism, both in private and in public.
- Janet McDonald for the great cover.
- Our students and fellow instructors at Superstars Writing Seminars for teaching us so much,

especially David Farland, Brandon Sanderson, Eric Flint, James A. Owen, and Tracy Hickman.

- Shannon & Linda Lifchez, for teaching us the concept of being "on stage" and polite at all times.
- Our friends, Kristine Kathryn Rusch & Dean Wesley Smith, Sarah & Dan Hoyt, Rebecca & Alan Lickiss, Amy Baxter, Doug Beason, Mike Resnick, Lisa & Tracy Mangum, Steven L. Sears, T. Duren Jones, Neil Peart, Brian Herbert, and Debra Ray, for always being there as sounding boards for us to bounce our ideas off of.
- The workshops and conferences that gave us the opportunity to refine our presentation: Nancy Knight and Dragon Con Writers' Track; Chris Mandeville and Pikes Peak Writers' Conference; Brisbane Writers' Festival; Jody Lynn Nye and her Writer's Two-Day Intensive Workshop; Life, the Universe, and Everything at Brigham Young University; Crested Butte Writers Conference; LDStorymakers, and others.
- Jason Chen at StoryBundle.com and NaNoWriMo (National Novel Writing Month) for helping us reach a much wider audience.
- Mark Lefebvre at Kobo for urging us to make this information available to all professionals.
- Our parents, Andy & Dorothy Anderson and Louis & Louise Moesta, for teaching us professionalism, kindness, and our work ethic.

About the Authors

Kevin J. Anderson has published over 125 books, more than fifty of which have been national or international bestsellers. He has written numerous novels in the Star Wars, X-Files, and Dune universes, as well as a unique steampunk fantasy novel, Clockwork Angels, based on the concept album by legendary rock group Rush. His original works include the Saga of Seven Suns series, the Terra Incognita fantasy trilogy, the Saga of Shadows trilogy, and his humorous horror series featuring Dan Shamble, Zombie PI. He has edited numerous anthologies, including the Five by Five and Blood Lite series.

Rebecca Moesta (pronounced MESS-tuh) wanted to be an author since her early teens, but it wasn't until 1991 that she began writing in earnest. Her solo novels include Buffy the Vampire Slayer: Little Things (2002) and three novels in the Junior Jedi Knights series. With her husband, Kevin J. Anderson, she wrote the Crystal Doors trilogy, the movie novelization of League of Extraordinary Gentlemen under the pseudonym "K.J. Anderson" (2003); a movie novelization of Supernova (2000); a novelization of the popular StarCraft computer game StarCraft: Shadow of the Xel'Naga, under the pseudonym "Gabriel Mesta" (2001); and a Star Trek graphic novel, The Gorn Crisis (2001). The team, currently working on Star Challengers, a Young Adult science fiction series, has also written two young adult Titan A.E. novels (2000), two high-tech Star Wars Pop-up Books, and the 14-book Young Jedi Knights series of Star Wars novels.

Together, they are the publishers of WordFire Press.

THE MILLION DOLLAR WRITING SERIES

Drawing on the Power of Resonance in Writing

Million Dollar Book Signings

Million Dollar Outlines

Million Dollar Productivity

Million Dollar Professionalism

The Non-User-Friendly Guide for Aspiring TV Writers

Made in the USA
Middletown, DE
19 May 2015